Losing It All & Finding Yourself

Richard W. Dortch

New Leaf Press

ISBN: 0-89221-239-X

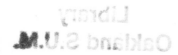

Contents

Dedication

to
Dr. and Mrs. Arthur Parsons

A certain man went down,
    fell, stripped and wounded.
He was left half-dead.
By chance a righteous person passed by.
Another looked on him and passed on the
    other side.
But a certain Samaritan came where he was.
When he saw him he had compassion on him.
He went to him, bound up his wounds,
    poured in oil and wine,
    and put him on his journey,
    and took care of him.
Which one of these three was a friend
    to him who fell?

Jesus said, "He that showed mercy on him."
(paraphrased)

I understand Jesus better now because of
Arthur and Usteena Parsons. They were, for me,
the Samaritans who helped restore my life and
ministry.

Preface

This book is unique. It contains a message you won't get anywhere else. You won't hear it on Phil Donohue or read about it in the *Wall Street Journal*. College professors and school textbooks don't include it in their course material. It's doubtful that you will hear anyone admit the kinds of things that you will read about in this book.

This message is not for the close-minded or the weak-willed. You may not need the truths found here until later, but at some point they will keep you from making a few of life's biggest mistakes.

This is preventive medicine from a man who has earned the right to speak on this topic. He lived a life of integrity for thirty-five years. Then, he put one foot over the edge and found himself careening down the slippery slope to destruction and failure. At the bottom, he landed among the debris of his own soiled reputation.

The name Richard Dortch is connected with PTL, Jim Bakker, and Heritage USA. It sounds familiar, doesn't it? As the former PTL president and television host, Richard Dortch was indicted in 1989 on charges of conspiracy and wire and mail fraud. Sentenced to eight years in a federal prison, this once highly respected pastor and leader of his denomination was labeled a convicted felon.

For the next eighteen months, Richard Dortch battled not only with his own guilt but for his life and health as well. Diagnosed with cancer that resulted in the loss of one kidney, he received an early release from prison.

The journey back began. With soul-searching honesty, Richard Dortch confronted himself and discovered the weak link in the chain. Like corroded metal, his integrity, now rusty and tarnished, had slowly been eaten away during the years at PTL. The silent process had gone unnoticed until it was too late.

How could he keep others from experiencing the slow, subtle erosion of their integrity? As the stages in the process became clear to him, he longed to share them with others — to somehow prevent them from making the same mistakes.

Let the message of this book sink deep into your heart and determine in your mind to be a person of integrity — whatever the cost.

Tim Dudley
Publisher

Introduction

As I came to the end of completing my second book, *Fatal Conceit,* I faced another turning point in my life. Pastors Larry and Pat Freeman of the Pinellas Park Wesleyan Church in Florida had reached out to us and really cared. He and his congregation were doing everything they could possibly do to encourage me and get me back to my calling. But there was another person and another place that I had to encounter. My dear friend, Pastor Ben Leonard, asked me to return to Granite City, Illinois, my hometown, the city where I was born and raised. It was the place of my beginnings, both as a person and as a Christian.

As soon as the pastor extended the invitation, I knew that God had something more in mind for me than simply delivering a sermon. Somehow I knew that in returning home, I was going to have an encounter with myself.

It was in Illinois where I had been chosen to be the state leader of our denomination. It was there that I had achieved so much of my life's work. I and others had kept the scorecard in my steps to success, but somewhere along the pathway, I lost it all.

Now I had to ask myself: *When I left my home-town, what went wrong? How could a boy raised in a steel mill town, in a very humble home and surround-ings, become involved in a national scandal?*

The Granite City church had sent out over 140 young people into the ministry. I was one of the few who had publicly failed. But most people really did not know what was going on in my heart.

Why did I lose my integrity and go to prison?

Why? That is the question.

I didn't have an answer before I went to prison, but I do now. I had to go back to the place where I lost myself in order to find myself — at the place of my beginnings.

I am reminded of Mary and Joseph. They went a full day's journey without Jesus before they noticed He was missing.

They lost Jesus in a day. They found Him after three days of frantic searching. It took three times longer to find Jesus than it did to lose Him.

It usually takes us much longer to regain what we have lost than it took for us to lose it in the first place.

After she found Jesus, Mary kept all these things in her heart. She knew in order never to lose Jesus again, she had to remember how she had lost Him the first time. Like Mary and Joseph, we can lose Jesus in the temple — at the place of our most spiritual activity. To find Him, we must go back to the place where we lost Him.

I lost it all. But on the way back, I found Jesus in a way I had never known Him before. Allow me to share with you from my heart what God has taught me on this difficult and painful journey.

1

Losing It All

In the summer of 1986, I received a telephone call from a man whom I believe is one of the few prophetic figures of our time — David Wilkerson. In fact, I considered him then, as I do now, to be more than just a "man of God." I believed he was a principled person who would not compromise his values. He was not for sale at any cost.

His telephone call caught me by surprise. After a few brief pleasantries, in a genuine straightforward fashion, he quickly addressed the issues on his heart.

He said, "Brother Dortch, I have been on a mountain seeking God's face and praying. In listening to the voice of the Lord, God has spoken to me. I have a word from the Lord. God will destroy PTL. The spirit of the Lord has departed from that place. But God is going to give you one last chance."

"It's not my ministry," I explained. "I'm not the head of this ministry."

"I know that. When I was in prayer, the Lord

told me to call you, Brother Dortch," he said solemnly. "*You* must do something, and it must be done quickly. What is going on at PTL is an abomination to God, and it must be stopped. Brother Dortch, you are the hope of getting some of these problems solved."

In a stunned manner, I responded, "You may well be right, but we need to hear it from you. I am certainly open to the possibility of your coming and sharing your vision with our entire staff."

Without responding to my invitation, he continued, "If something isn't done quickly, God is going to write *ICHABOD* over the doors of Heritage USA. The birds are going to be flying in that hotel within a year — unless something is done and there is true repentance."

I implored him to come, but he said it would be impossible at that time. I pleaded with him to meet with Jim Bakker and/or me. He encouraged me to address the staff myself.

"Won't you please come and tell us what you feel? Would you meet with Jim and me?" I begged, my tone becoming more and more insistent.

At the time David Wilkerson called, Jim Bakker was in California. I did my best to get Brother David to come and unburden his soul to us, but he felt that he could not do it.

Warnings

I called an entire staff meeting for the next Friday afternoon at 2:30 p.m. Everyone was to be released from their jobs and assemble at the PTL television studio.

By that Friday, Jim Bakker had returned from

California, and I shared with him David Wilkerson's prophetic word. I told him about the scheduled meeting and asked him to introduce me that day before I spoke. I wanted the staff to know that Jim Bakker was standing with me in what I had to say. Jim cheerfully responded and said he would be glad to do so.

I addressed the staff that Friday afternoon in a way I had never done before at Heritage USA. I dealt with every known sin that I felt God leading me to address, including infidelity in marriage, adultery, homosexuality, drinking, pornography, conversation, and language. I discussed the importance of paying our tithes and living a life pleasing to God. I felt it was necessary to cover the fundamentals of Christian living and the conduct expected of believers.

"Our partners and viewers have a right to expect every one of us to have proper moral values in harmony with our Christian witness," I told the PTL staff. "They have a right to expect us to live an overcoming life — a life above reproach."

At the conclusion of my message, a holy silence hovered over the auditorium.

Upon returning to the dressing room, Jim remarked to me, "If there's anything you missed today, I don't know what it was. And it all needed to be said."

In my soul I felt that I had delivered the message that, in a sense, had been laid upon someone else's heart. But it was a message I knew had to be communicated.

I then called David Wilkerson and pleaded with him once again to meet with us. He reluctantly consented to meet with Jim Bakker and me on the following Thursday in Chattanooga or Knoxville, Tennessee. The next morning, however, his secretary phoned to say he would be unable to come. I was extremely disappointed.

Other Christians were also sending warnings to PTL. Some of them, without fanfare, privately attempted to lay a foundation on which to get our attention. They were unsuccessful. I'm not sure we wanted to listen to anyone.

As the year progressed, the rumors, stories, and allegations concerning Jim Bakker and a woman continued. I found myself frequently trying to answer the questions that were coming, never imagining the whole matter would explode in our faces.

Losing It All

Within one year of David Wilkerson's phone call I was fired from my position as executive director of PTL Ministries, and my wife and I were forced to move from our home in Charlotte, North Carolina.

For two and one-half years I lived in torment! What was to happen to us? Every day I hastened to read the newspapers, *USA Today*, the *Washington Post*, the *New York Times*, and the *St. Petersburg Times*. What was happening to me? It was on all the major television networks each night. When the indictments came it was as if execution day had arrived for us. We lived in a dark place of pain.

We lost almost everything. My money went to cover legal fees. My denomination revoked my ministerial credentials. Friends whom I had known for years neither phoned nor wrote.

I lost my integrity, my reputation, my freedom, and my sense of self-respect. Prison robbed me of privacy, my family, and my income. I lost it all.

After serving eighteen months I was released from prison to go to a halfway house for five months. The cancer had cost me a kidney. I was not well. I walked with a cane for almost one year, but I began my journey back.

Over the next year there were many turning points. One in particular brought God's purpose for my life into clear focus.

Don George, pastor of Calvary Temple in the Dallas/Ft. Worth metroplex, invited me to speak to his congregation and guests. I knew Pastor George very well. He had been a true friend to my wife and me down through the years. His congregation had always received us warmly in the past. I had spoken at Calvary Temple many times before they built their beautiful, mammoth cathedral, and later participated in the dedication of their completed facility.

During the two months prior to my scheduled engagement at Calvary anxiety had gripped me almost every day. The thought was constantly on my mind that the Christian Booksellers Association's annual convention was being held in Dallas at the same time. I was filled with fear at the thought of speaking before many nationally known ministers, business persons, authors, singers, and television personalities who would be in the service.

But it was more than that. I knew this was not

going to be just an encounter with a congregation or even well-known Christian ministers and celebrities. This was going to be an encounter with me. An encounter I had to face sooner or later.

Unfinished Business

When the day arrived and we were driving to the church I wondered, *Would there be the crowd I was expecting?* Perhaps only the local congregation would know I was going to speak.

My hopes dissipated as we came to the freeway exit for the church. There before us loomed a giant marquee announcing Richard Dortch as that morning's guest speaker. Most of the convention attendees would surely have seen the sign on their way in from the airport. There was no hope of escape now.

Immediately I knew what I had to do. I was "made to know" — this is the way I describe God's revelations to me — that I must confess my sins and ask forgiveness, apologizing to the people in the church that morning for the hurt and reproach I had brought on the gospel. I knew that was the right thing to do, and with God's grace I could do it.

The members and Pastor George lovingly greeted Mildred and me as we made our way into the church. After a few choruses and the opening prayer, I stood to my feet and, with trembling knees and breaking heart, approached the pulpit.

"Pastor George," I began, my voice barely above a whisper, "thank you for your kind introduction, but please stay here at the pulpit with me. There is some unfinished business I need to do before I speak."

Silence filled the cathedral. I could sense the audience's waiting for my next word.

"This church," I continued, "has been a friend to Mildred and me for many years. I hurt you, Pastor. I brought shame to my friends, this church, and the body of Christ. I brought reproach to you as a person and to this group of people, and for this I am very sorry. I ask each of you to forgive me, and I plead with this congregation to forgive me. I know God has forgiven me, but now I need to ask you to forgive me because I so regret the pain I brought into your lives."

As I ceased talking, I felt as if time itself had stopped. The audience appeared stunned by my confession. All the respected people I had expected to be there were seated throughout the church that morning. Yet, through God's grace, I faced my sins and publicly confessed the things I had done wrong.

I waited for what seemed like an eternity, then I heard a sob, and then another. Someone stood and began to weep. Then I felt the warm arm of Pastor George around me. With tears, he hugged me intensely, whispering, "You are forgiven." At that moment I was lost in a world of love.

When I regained my composure, the congregation was standing, some applauding, some weeping. I looked at them through my tears, wondering what had just happened and what would happen next.

After a few minutes, the people quieted down, and Pastor George stepped to the microphone. "Richard Dortch," he said, looking directly into my eyes, "you are forgiven. We want you to know the peace we have all found. Never again to this congregation need you say anything about the past. We forgive you, just as we have been forgiven. You are loved."

The majesty of the moment was overwhelming. Not the majesty of my being center stage, or in front of many of the mighty men and women of faith I knew and respected. The majesty of that moment came from within. It came as I asked forgiveness for my sins.

I had lost it all, but I was finding my way back.

Confronting Myself

After my confession before the believers of Calvary Church, I determined that, if I must go before every congregation that invites me to speak and confess my failure, I would do it.

Although confessing my sin and asking and receiving forgiveness brought great healing to my heart and mind, I knew the process was not complete. I needed to do more than confess to others; I needed to confront myself. I knew I had to search my soul to discover the reasons for my transgressions and downfall.

After many months of self-examination and near total despair, I identified the root of my sin: I had violated the power entrusted to me by God and by my brothers and sisters in the faith. I had tried to seize some of God's glory, and He would have none of it.

God shares His glory with no one, but I had wanted some attention. I had wanted acclamation. I had wanted power to do with as I pleased. I got all of that along with a good dose of chastisement and humiliation.

From the time I stepped down as superintendent of my denomination in Illinois to take the position with the PTL ministry until the day I was released from prison, more than five years had passed. During that time I constantly faced the issue of how the violation of power had eroded the integrity I had spent a lifetime building.

What is Integrity?

During the long months that I was in prison, I had a lot of time to think. Over and over again, I asked myself, *What is integrity? Is it the same as honesty and morality? Or is it more than that?*

As I read the newspapers and watched the evening news during those longs days at Eglin Federal Prison Camp, I saw countless reports of men and women who had compromised their integrity and now found themselves the objects of media attention. I began to realize that, in today's world, true integrity often eludes us. The loss of integrity, however, raises its ugly head from every corner of our society. What has gone wrong?

A prime-time news telecast exposes the fund-raising and spending practices of television ministries and well-known evangelists, sending shock waves throughout the evangelical community.

Reports surface that Stanford and several other prestigious universities admit they took government money — taxpayers' dollars — and fraudulently used it.

Accusations of impropriety in the relationship of priests to their followers surface regularly, embarrassing the Catholic Church and tarnishing its image.

Forty-seven scientists at the Harvard and Emery University Medical Schools are accused of producing hyped and falsified scientific research.

The savings and loan fiasco, the House bank rubber-check debacle, the junk bonds swindle — all these make one wonder: If news reporters, government workers, bank executives, office holders, church leaders, university professors, and the business community have no scruples, does anyone have integrity anymore?

This question involves much more than just an occasional evangelist having an illicit affair, or Ivan Boesky stealing money from Wall Street, or a *Washington Post* writer making up the story for which she received a Pulitzer prize. It involves people from all walks of life — those involved in the work of the church and those in the secular community.

It's easy for us to point fingers at Jimmy Swaggart and forget the tens of thousands of other ministers — and lay people — whose private sins have not yet been exposed. The problem also extends beyond Jim Baker and Richard Dortch of the PTL scandal. It involves all of us.

How honest are *you* ?

A House subcommittee estimated recently that one out of every three working Americans alters their educational or career credentials in order to get hired for a job.

What's going on? Are the American people dishonest?

A survey indicates that 91 percent of the American people lie regularly.

Those same people, however, are firm in their

conviction that "others" — up to and including public officials — should be held to high standards of honesty.

Seven out of ten Americans say the president of the United States should never tell a lie. At least that's the conviction of the 91 percent who admit that they regularly lie. But who knows if they're telling the truth?

About 50 percent of us go to church each week, and 45 percent of all Americans say that we are born-again Christians. That's hard to believe when 91 percent admit they are liars.[1]

John Gardner, founder of the Common Cause, recently said, "Duplicity and deception, in public and private life, are substantially greater than they have been in the past."

Reverend Theodore Hesburgh, former president of the University of Notre Dame, stated, "To the extent family life is disintegrating, kids are not being taught values about lying, cheating, and stealing."

When a New York City school student turned in a purse she had found, complete with the $1,000 cash, not a single school official congratulated her on her virtue. Her teacher explained, "If I come from a position of what is right and wrong, then I am no longer their counselor."

The apparent translation: We no longer believe in black and white, only shades of gray.

Twentieth century Americans have grown cautious about making value judgments. There is a growing degree of cynicism and sophistication in our society — a sense that all things are relative and nothing is absolutely right or wrong.

Paul Harvey, the noted news commentator, recently observed that Sears, one of America's great retail institutions, lost $48 million in one quarter to shrinkage. Most retailers agree that the greatest loss in shrinkage is due to theft.

Who's doing the stealing? It's a known fact that retail *employees* steal four times more than the public takes through shoplifting. Why? Because a store or place of business is impersonal; it's easier to steal from "the store" than to put a gun to a clerk's head.

Most Americans believe dishonesty is inherit in business practices today. The philosophy seems to be, "Do whatever is necessary to succeed and beat the competition."

"People feel like suckers if they're honest," a recent article in a *Business News* magazine reported.

People Who Could Do No Wrong

What gives me, Richard Dortch, someone who lost his integrity, the right to raise questions about truth and honesty? That's a valid question.

I have paid an immense price for my loss of integrity and learned how easily it can be forfeited. I don't want you to make the same mistakes.

The men I met in prison were not the kind I expected. Many were professional people who would be considered the most unlikely to fall victim to their crimes.

Among my fellow inmates were lawyers; executives serving time for bank fraud; administrators involved in savings and loan scandals; medical doctors who had not told the truth about their Medicare and Medicaid funds. I shared a prison dormitory with a former Secret Service agent, a judge, and men who had been government officials and county prosecutors. In fact, I wasn't the only former churchman serving time either; six other ministers were incarcerated during my prison term.

What caused the downfall of these men who had so much going for them?

It is said that adversity tests our ability to survive, and prosperity tests our integrity. That's when some of us failed the test — when we were at our peak and had it all. How did that happen? Most fell blindly into the snare, unaware that the primrose path was strewn with subtle booby traps.

Where are these pitfalls hidden? Within the day to day decisions that each of us must make — decisions involving different kinds of integrity. In the chapters that follow, we will consider integrity from four vantage points:

1. The Arrogance of Integrity
2. Selective Integrity
3. Judgmental Integrity
4. Consensual Integrity

Maybe you will find yourself before it's too late.

2

The Arrogance of Integrity

We have all been told — at one time or another — that our good name is our most valuable asset. A commendation from our boss or the adoration of people reinforces the notion that we are building a good reputation.

While we might tolerate certain accusations against the things we do, we will not stand for attacks on our character or our good name. To a point, this is admirable, but there is a subtle temptation that lies just beneath the surface of this sort of motivation.

Once our reputation grows among the circles in which we live, travel, work, or worship, that distinction begins to take on a life of its own. A certain synergy develops that allows us to think more highly of ourselves than is safe to do.

The Scriptures warned us — many centuries ago — that this sort of pride produces the perfect setting for failure.

King David returned victorious from battle and, with great presumption, looked upon another woman.

The apostle Peter shared a meal with his Lord and boldly proclaimed that he would follow Him until death. Before the morning sun, Peter broke that vow.

The Book of Proverbs warns, "The Lord detests all the proud of heart. Be sure of this: They will not go unpunished" (Prov. 16:5).

James writes, "God opposes the proud but gives grace to the humble" (James 4:6). These words are not written for someone else but for us.

The Root of Arrogance

After I took the job as an executive at PTL, I began to realize that my reputation had preceded me. I heard people say, "We can quit worrying about that place now. Richard Dortch is there, and he wouldn't put up with anything that would be dishonest, illegal, or wrong. He will have a straight-arrow, squeaky-clean operation."

When I went to my new job at Heritage USA, I *was* Mr. Clean. I believed, as did others, that nothing could go wrong. I was proud of the fact that in thirty-five years of public life, there had never been a rumor or scandal attached to me.

I had never made a "deal" with anyone.

I didn't have an adulterous relationship in my past.

I had not stolen money or anything else.

I was proud of my reputation.

People had told me over and over, "Everything will be above board with you there." I believed their assessment because that's the way I had operated throughout my entire career as a pastor and church executive. I was above it all. Or, so I thought.

Slowly, however, I began to believe that what others said about me and my reputation was not only true, but something I could depend on to prevent any questionable dealings. As the ministry at PTL began to grow rapidly, my confidence in my own integrity blurred my need for humility before the Lord. I became arrogant in my integrity and lost sight of the big picture.

Paul Cedar, a respected pastor, wrote about the danger we face in this dilemma:

> Pride tells us to go it alone; God tells us to go with Him.
>
> Pride tells us to follow our instincts; God tells us to follow Him.
>
> Pride tells us to utilize human knowledge and rational approaches; God tells us to acknowledge Him.
>
> Pride tells us to "fake it;" God tells us to allow the truth to set us free.
>
> Pride tells us never to appear weak or uncertain; God tells us that His strength is made perfect in our weakness.
>
> Pride tells us to have people focus upon us; God tells us to invite people to follow us with their eyes upon Jesus![1]

The Outcome of Arrogance

The arrogance of integrity is blind. As a result,

I couldn't see what was going on around me. Because I took satisfaction in what others had said about my integrity, that still, small voice that warns of danger could no longer be clearly heard. It had been drowned out by the roar of "what's being done for the Lord." I was not listening to the umpire of my heart.

I became so intoxicated with the growth of Heritage USA and so enamored with what was developing around me that I refused to see beyond my own circle of responsibility. The sins of adultery, fornication, and embezzlement were so far removed from me that I felt confident in my own morality.

Being on television, speaking to adoring crowds, and having favorable articles written about me fed my ego. I thought that, because of my character, nothing could happen to me. What accusation could possibly be made?

Besides, I had always prided myself on being able to size up situations and pinpoint problems effectively. While everyone else pondered over what appeared to be the dilemma, I was able to perceive what *wasn't* being said. I knew that's where the root of the problem could be found.

At PTL, however, I was too proud to permit myself to face the reality of the situation.

This kind of arrogance of integrity is not the exclusive sin of church leaders. It is natural to man, regardless of his profession. The temptation to believe that your strength comes from yourself is alluring.

Mark Ritchie, a successful commodities trader, by his own confession, fell victim to his own arrogance:

It wasn't just the realization that I genuinely thought myself better than others, but it was the fact that my goal in life was to improve myself to the point that it would, in fact, be true; so I could, with honesty, face myself in the mirror and say that I was good, better, maybe even best — all relative terms that can only be defined in relation to other people. Even then, some objective measurement must be employed; quantity of money, power, influence, sexual attractiveness. Incongruous as it seemed, my life goal was to become stuck on myself, the very thing everyone agreed to be the worst of qualities.[2]

Almost weekly the media brings another revelation about a high-ranking official or well-known personality who — previously considered invincible — has committed a fatal error.

A respected savings and loan executive is found guilty of violating the trust of his shareholders and depositors. Members of the United States Senate are implicated in the matter.

Did they set out to defraud? Probably not.

When arrogance about our own reputation and integrity dominates our life, then we get out of sync and wrong decisions are inevitable.

Robert Linder, professor of history at Kansas State University, has analyzed United States presidents and found that an arrogance of one's own integrity can result in duplicity:

Ulysses Simpson Grant (1869-77), for example, attended services with considerable regularity with his devout wife at the Metropolitan Methodist Church in Washington. When as president he was requested by the *Sunday School Times* to compose a message for its readers, he advised, "Hold fast to the Bible as the sheet anchor of your liberties; write its precepts in your hearts and practice them in your lives."

Although relatively honest, Grant allowed corruption to run rampant during his eight years as president.[3]

Church leaders, business executives, politicians, professionals, and people from all walks of life, must guard against this subtle temptation. Few people, if any, start out with the intent to fail or disappoint others. In an effort to achieve their goals and make their organizations successful, they choose a demanding responsibility.

It is for that very reason — because their original intentions were good and honorable — that arrogance becomes such a personal enemy.

Steven Covey, in his *The Seven Habits of Highly Effective People*, underscores the importance of an uncompromised integrity within ourselves:

. . . Integrity is, fundamentally, the value we place on ourselves. It's our ability to make and keep commitments to ourselves, to "walk our talk." In other words, if you are an effective manager of yourself, your discipline comes from within; it is a function of your independent will. You are a disciple, a follower of your own deep values and their source. And you have the will, the integrity, to subordinate your feelings, your impulses, your moods, to those values.[4]

The psalmist David said, "Do not lift up your horn on high, do not speak with insolent pride" (Ps. 75:5).

God simply states, don't toot your own horn, and don't let anyone else toot it. Whether you are in the valley or on the mountain, the tilt of the neck should always be the same. You have to look up to see God.

God takes, and God gives away. God raises up or brings down. We are not nearly as important as we sometimes think we are.

Guarding Against Arrogance

Reflecting back, I realize that I felt, because my reputation was spotless, it would protect me. I only focused on issues that were obvious and forgot about the trivial indiscretions that were swirling all around me. I set aside the fact that life, as a whole, is made up of the little things.

As an administrator at PTL, I taught, believed, and practiced a very simple philosophy about integrity: "If we can do what we are proposing and explain it to our supporters and feel totally comfortable in doing it, it's probably the right thing to do. If we have to remain silent on it or compartmentalize it, it's probably wrong, and we'll suffer if we do it." I regret that I didn't follow my own advice.

I have never accused anyone of having committed my sin, and I bear no responsibility to accept the blame for others. But we must universally understand that the problem of integrity involves all of us. Without question, it is the issue of the nineties.

Many won't realize what is going on in their own personal lives — until it's too late. They don't sense how deep they have sunk: telling lies, implying untruths, cheating on their income tax, taking money or anything that is not theirs, being unfaithful to their spouse, doing things to hurt others, not doing what they should have done, coveting someone else's possessions, and having a multitude of gods.

The arrogance of integrity is the result of pride that begins to take root in the life of someone who has earned a reputation for integrity. It is borne out of a failure to realize daily that what the Bible says about people is true of us all — our flesh is constantly seeking to fulfill itself in pride.

Arrogance, pride, and a haughty spirit always come before the fall.

How do we guard against this dilemma?

First, we must remember that we are never more right with God than when we admit we are wrong. The grace of our Lord — and not our good work — is His response to our need.

It's difficult to come forward and say, "I was wrong. I have sinned! What I did or didn't do was wrong, and I am sorry. Please forgive me."

Integrity, however, requires completeness. I must know in my heart that I have done everything that I can do to admit my errors, acknowledge my sins, and ask for forgiveness. Then I will know "there is now no condemnation to them that are in Christ Jesus . . . who walk not after the flesh, but after the spirit" (Rom. 8:1-4).

During the PTL investigation, a law enforcement officer told me, "I was surprised that you were as forthcoming as you have been." That confirmed to me that I had told the truth. I was free! It is wonderful to know there are no secrets lurking about still to be revealed or concealed facts not yet told.

Secondly, we all need a select group of people to whom we are totally accountable. This group does not have to be large or influential, rather they must simply care enough about you to tell you what you need to hear.

Integrity in its simplest form means wholeness, completeness, entirety. It comes from a root word that means intact. Integrity means that our heart is not divided; there is no hidden agenda. Loving and honest relationships provide a haven of safety and security from the arrogance of integrity.

3

Selective Integrity

"You can't ask me to leave my position as the leader now, we're having the most successful time we've ever had here." That is what a top official at PTL said to me when I confronted him about his apparent problem — a problem everyone acknowledged except him.

Almost every person that I can think of who has fallen — whether layman or minister — did so because they believed they were the exception. They thought they could pick and choose when and how to sin. They could sin — even if only occasionally and for a good cause — and it would make no difference. Their public persona portrayed what they wanted everyone to believe was true about them. They convinced themselves that no one would ever see the other side of their life.

A prominent broadcast executive recently told me, "The biggest motivator in Christian television is the checkbook. It has less to do with the purpose and will of God than revenue — who pays the most gets in the mainstream of the 'will of God.' The time slot opens up for those who have the checkbook. Our soul is for sale. When will we learn that God's economy is not ours? Once your persona overshadows your ministry, it is as if you are waving your alms before men. Therefore, you have your reward."

Yes, money was a factor in the way we thought and the decisions we made at PTL. There were occasions when the greater good took second place to the money that was involved.

No wonder the Master of our souls said, "The love of money is the root of all evil" (1 Tim. 6:10).

When greed gets into our spirit, we are usually the last ones to know. Others can see it, but we can't.

When you're living close to God, He has a way of rubbing off on you. When your affections are on money, it, too, has a way of rubbing off and dirtying your hands. Too late, some of us discover it's not worth it.

Self-denial is the best and wisest course.

God Understands

Some people are good at correcting the errors of others — and that can be helpful — but they don't recognize the iniquity in themselves. They thunder to their children, "Don't you cheat!" Yet they steal office supplies and bring them home from work.

What is selective integrity? It's the idea that: *If others do it, it's wrong; if I do it, God understands.* When we expect and demand more of others than we deliver ourselves, we set ourselves up as little gods. The sin of selective integrity tempts us all.

Americans have developed a passion for the scoop on public figures. It doesn't matter whether they are politicians or pastors. If someone has a picture, a tape, or an eyewitness — people want to know.

This seeming demand for high morality would be a welcome trend if it reflected a concern that *all* of us should be more conscious of our actions. Sadly, most polls indicate that we demand one standard of others and quite another of ourselves. Some actions have been labeled taboo, while others are acceptable — if we can get away with them.

The pastor who abhors infidelity might think nothing of cheating on his tax statement. The extra income he received in December can be rationalized away as not taxable — or even reportable on the 1040 form.

The politician who speaks openly in opposition to homosexual behavior may have no qualms about violating his own marriage vows.

In fact, most of us have become so good at selective integrity that our attitudes reflect it.

A recent study found that most Americans agree that the American family spends less time together and is in trouble as a result, but the respondents thought their own families were okay. So where are the families with problems? It's always the neighbors next door — never us.

This selective integrity leads to a life of extreme self-centeredness. David Halberstam, writer and journalist, described this attitude in his book, *The Next Century:*

Not surprisingly, most Americans, faced with a new equation, wanted it both ways. They wanted a sort of no-fault patriotism — to keep enjoying the far greater personal freedoms and entitlements of the seventies and eighties with the vastly improved lifestyle and greater professional possibilities, while their neighbors were to revert to the more disciplined lives of the fifties. We were, in effect, a great free people, anxious for everyone to start making sacrifices, except, of course, ourselves.[1]

The late Joseph Fletcher caused quite a stir when he wrote his controversial work on situation ethics. To many he seemed to be promoting the notion that lying was acceptable, perhaps even honorable, if it served some higher good.

The idea of selective integrity was certainly not original with Fletcher, but his book proved to be a watershed on legitimizing the subject.

Former Nixon advisor, Chuck Colson, found himself in the middle of our nation's most devastating integrity crisis — Watergate. A few years later, when it was announced that Colson was born again, many people, including some Christians, were skeptical.

After a decade and a half, however, his testimony has borne fruit. In a recent publication, *Kingdoms in Conflict*, Colson reflects on how the Nixon White House would use the White House church services for political rather than spiritual purposes:

People in power use power to keep themselves in power. Even if they are genuinely interested in a special interest group's agenda — or naturally disposed to their position — they will work that relationship for everything they can get out of it.[2]

The weekly church services Nixon scheduled most Sundays for the East Room provided great opportunities as well. To select the preacher, we determined who would give us the greatest impact — politically, that is, not spiritually. At the time I was a nominal Christian at best, and had no way to judge the spiritual. And there were always two hundred or more seats to be filled, tickets that were like keys to the political kingdoms.[3]

What's Best for Me?

The practice of selective integrity has long been suspected in business as the tension between profits and people stretches integrity to the max.

In the eighties, business schools enjoyed record enrollments as young people started on their climb up the ladder. When how much money you made became the barometer of success, being totally profit driven no longer held a negative stigma. As the generation of greedy graduates replaced the more traditional executives, climbing the corporate ladder meant stepping on anyone who got in your way and grabbing as much as you could carry.

At the same time, the American marketplace was threatened by overseas competition, a shrinking consumer base, and a growing emphasis on quality. These changes became a challenge for corporate leaders who had to choose between what was best for business, stockholders, employees, or themselves.

While pursuing integrity on many fronts, they often selectively chose areas where they could personally profit without getting caught.

Tom Peters, celebrated management consultant, illustrates one example of selective integrity:

> To use the psychologist's terms, integrity is not only absolute (stealing is bad, period), but it involves "perceived equity." That is, fairness is in the eye of the beholder. Paying bonuses to management and withholding worker bonuses in a problematic year is perceived to be unfair, regardless of the extenuating circumstances.[4]

Peters goes on to conclude that integrity may be far more important in the smaller areas of an executive's life:

> Integrity may be about little things as much as or more than big ones. It's about executives taking friends, rather than customers, to sit in the company's box seats at the ballpark. It's about pushing salespeople at the end quarter to place orders, knowing that many will

be canceled within the week — but that
the cancellations will count in the next
period for accounting purposes.[5]

Such action has not, however, gone unnoticed. Litigation against business executives for
breach of integrity has been on the rise in recent
years. The rash of legal activity on Wall Street
concerning insider trading and fraud has become
legend.

Were these business leaders untrustworthy?
Did they lie or cheat in every area of their life? No,
they selectively chose areas where the potential
return was the greatest when compared to the risk
of being caught.

Cooking the Books

The private sector has not been alone in pursuing selective integrity. And, while such action is
reprehensible anywhere, it can be no more frightening than when it occurs in government.

Government leaders serve in a sacred trust
with the electorate. In America that trust is considered essential to a democracy. Local, state, and
national leaders swear to uphold their respective
constitutions. When government's integrity is
called into question, the future of our culture is at
stake.

Sadly, in the past two decades one leader after
another, from both parties, has been accused of
swearing to an oath one day and breaching integrity the next. Alvin Toffler put the deceptive practice of "cooking the books" into a contemporary
perspective:

Governments, of course, have been "cooking their books" at least since the invention of double-entry ledgers by the Venetians in the fourteenth century. They have been "cooking" all sorts of data, information, and knowledge, not just budgetary or financial, since Day One. What's new is the ability to fry, broil, or microwave the stuff with the help of computers.[6]

Integrity says that we must not lie, but selective integrity says that the only real test of a lie is whether or not people are enraged by a particular deception or a distortion that they have learned.

Is it any wonder that our nation is so soundly confused on the issue of selectivity in our integrity?

President Reagan vows that he knew nothing about the Iran-Contra deal involving trading American arms for hostages. But who believes him? A web of misinformation and half-truths make it clear that high officials in our government were deceiving each other and the public — and perhaps themselves.

The humorous Mark Shal said, "George Washington said, 'I cannot tell a lie.' Richard Nixon could not tell the truth. Ronald Reagan couldn't tell the difference."

The problem of selective integrity has become epidemic in public life. Sadly, if something is pervasive enough for long enough, it can be accepted as the norm.

But there is hope. The American public appears to be fed up with the lies. According to *U.S.*

News and World Report, 70 percent of the American people are dissatisfied with the current standards of honesty.

A crisis of confidence exists in most areas of life today because selective integrity is being practiced.

Sending Mixed Signals

Each time we experience selective integrity, whether as the one who is doing it or being harmed by it, something happens inside us. I believe we lose respect for each other and, ultimately, ourselves.

Peters suggests that we cannot view these as mere lapses:

> These minor lapses set a tone of disrespect for people, products, systems, customers, distributors, and relationships that can readily become pervasive. That is, there is no such thing as a minor lapse in integrity.[7]

In the maelstrom that affected all of us at PTL, I've heard others define precisely what happened to me there. The stories reported by the news media were totally untrue, yet they were repeated as fact.

When asked if they are persons of integrity, these same reporters respond quickly, "Of course!" Do they tell the truth? No, the story was simply too juicy for them not to mention, whether or not it was true.

Truth cannot be selective. That is how integrity is lost.

We all do it. When we flatter people to achieve our own purposes, we are being dishonest with them and with ourselves.

Selective integrity is the hypocrisy of knowing that there is duplicity in our lives. It is saying to someone, "I sure do love you," when we know in our heart that we seldom, if ever, think of him and have never cared enough to help him in any way.

It is making up our minds about something or someone, and then going out and looking for facts to prove what we have already decided.

Integrity is telling the truth and not picking and choosing our facts. Selective integrity, however, is doing evil and expecting good to come from it.

In recent days when someone has said to me, "I certainly do love you," I have restrained my spirit and thought to myself, "I do hope that you don't treat everyone you love the way you have demonstrated your love to me."

Selective integrity sends mixed signals to people. In one moment we are pledging our covenant of commitment, and in the next we're turning on them. Using selective integrity, you can tell the truth with the intent of leaving the impression of something other than the truth you have spoken.

Staying Accountable

Selective integrity is common to us all. While we may hold truth with passion in one area, there are other times when we wink, or worse yet, close both eyes.

For many of us the yellow light has been blinking in our minds for a long time. Then the red light comes on, and in our mad rush to tell our story, picking and choosing, we forged straight ahead. We knew it was wrong, but we thought we would not be caught.

When we are trying to develop a philosophy about right and wrong by picking and choosing, we need to pull back and listen to our hearts.

What can we do to guard our hearts?

Like the issue of arrogance, an accountability group is vital. The first line of defense against selective integrity, however, is with those closest to us — our spouse, our children, our work associates.

We must create an environment at home and at work where others sense it is all right to point out any area where, they feel, we are sending mixed signals. I know this is risky, but the one who ultimately loses the most in selective integrity is the one practicing it.

The benefit of a more open environment at home and at work pays a valuable dividend. When I must be accountable for all of my actions, then, as Paul wrote to the Corinthians, "The power of Christ can rest upon me" (2 Cor. 12:9).

4

Judgmental Integrity

When a leader, no matter his position, whether private or public, business or profession, clergy or layman, begins to harshly judge the actions of others, he may simply be trying to drown his own guilt. Preachers, politicians, and the media have been accused of judgmental integrity. They decry sin in the community while carrying on a secret affair or practicing dishonesty.

I recall a well-known television evangelist who, with fiery indignation, preached against pornography. After many years of fruitful ministry, however, his hypocrisy was revealed when he was caught with a prostitute and a car full of pornographic magazines.

The same scene can be repeated each week in communities across America. Maybe you heard about the minister who rallied against gay rights in Florida but was later arrested for soliciting sex from an undercover policeman.

Judgmental integrity is practiced just as fearlessly in non-sexual settings. Tom Peters describes the boss who brags about service on one hand, while acting hypocritically:

> The boss who preaches quality, but puts wholly unrealistic schedule demands on the plant of operational center, is seen as a hypocrite. Trust, integrity, fairness in dealing with others (all under the gun to do unrealistic things and sign up for unrealistic promises), and quality/service all go kaput.[1]

Over the past century, America has witnessed a tug of war between labor and management borne out of mutual mistrust. Both sides demand that the other practice impeccable integrity, but neither side will trust the other to carry through without a contract.

One of America's largest airlines went first into bankruptcy and then into demise. The union accused management (specifically, the ownership) of siphoning off profits for other ventures while demanding 100 percent of time and effort from labor. Did management know their actions would bankrupt the company and rob long time employees of future benefits? Yes, union leaders argue.

As the world grows smaller and information becomes more pervasive, the double standard practiced by governments around the world is becoming painfully obvious. Nowhere has this been more explosive than in Eastern Europe. For almost a half century leaders in places like Romania demanded loyalty from the people and fidelity to the law of government. The overt immorality of Western type dress, music, and movies was officially prohibited and offenders swiftly punished.

As Romania's economy faltered, however, and hundreds of thousands of people began to starve, the people grew restless. Food shortages made the people wary of the government's promises.

When the dictatorship of Romania was toppled and their leader executed, the horrible truth came out — first to the people of Romania and then, through Western news agencies, to the rest of the world. While children starved to death in orphanages, the government leaders had lived like millionaires and feasted on imported delicacies.

The anger and resentment of being judged harshly by a government that practiced its own secret sins was the fuel for revolution. In country after country throughout eastern Europe, people demanded the truth. And those who lived by the sword began to die by the sword.

Here, in America, the situation has not reached this crisis point — yet. There is, however, a growing resentment against those in authority who have been holding the American people accountable while playing by a different set of rules themselves.

The media scoop that members of Congress were writing bad checks at the House bank was followed closely by the revelation that some members had failed to pay their tab at the Congressional Restaurant. At first, Americans seemed to respond with more ridicule than anything else. The story made great fodder for the late night comedians.

As the nineties settled in, however, pollsters reported that Americans were getting fed up with incumbents and their perceived hypocrisy. In Tampa, a rally entitled "Throw the rascals (incumbents) out" drew a record crowd. As a result, President Bush's popularity began to plummet despite a previous record of confidence from the American people.

Finger Pointing

As soon as the PTL disaster hit my life, the voices started crying out, and I knew the finger pointing had begun.

It was interesting to sit back and note the people who were the meanest and the least redemptive. Often harsh and inaccurate, their statements captured the attention of the media. Today, some of those people are no longer in the Lord's work. The true character of their lives — unknown to me but revealed by the Almighty — surfaced later.

When our concern for integrity is rooted in covering up our own misdeeds rather than for the benefit of truth to everyone, we have become judgmental.

The Greatest Man who ever lived asked the question, "How wilt thou say to thy brother, Let me pull out the mote out of thine eye; and, behold, a beam is in thine own eye?" (Matt. 7:4). Most people know that a mote is just a tiny piece of dust or a speck of material that can get in your eye. A beam, obviously, is a support, either wood or metal, that holds up the roof of a building.

Jesus said, "Can't you see that?"

The person who finger points actually thinks that darkness is light, and they don't know the difference. That's why deterioration sets in.

When we fantasize that we are something we are not, the question of our own integrity becomes an immense problem. "If we say that we have no sin, we deceive ourselves, and the truth is not in us" (1 John 1:8). Somehow we must learn to step back and listen to our hearts and deal very severely with ourselves. Otherwise, a judgmental attitude will let us lie to ourselves, believe it, and begin to point fingers at others.

In our quest to straighten out the world and to correct those we target, we lose the sense of what we have become ourselves. We see nothing wrong in what we are doing. We hardly recognize the darkness in which we are walking. When such a spirit grasps us, we are determined to conquer and enslave someone else.

How often have we wounded a loved one or slain our enemies by our negative comments (that we were not certain were true)? This kind of attitude reflects much more about ourselves than those we are trying to judge.

Like a bomb waiting to detonate, judgmental integrity explodes, delivering a blow to the innocent. When the smoke clears, the recipient of our criticism stands condemned.

A judgmental concept of integrity allows a spirit into our hearts that loathes, detests, and despises people. When we get carried away in our own importance, jealousy and envy also play a part. Then, instead of healing, we inflict further injury to the wounded brother or sister.

We must always ask ourselves, before jumping into a matter: Are we attempting to slay our foe or bring help, hope, and healing? That's a choice each of us must face. We must seek to arbitrate our spirits, not go off in haste and bring hurt to the community of our fellows.

"Always leave something to build on" is the admonition I heard as a young executive from a very wise man.

Each of us has a Referee who adjudicates right and wrong and makes the choices. That Person, however, is not us.

Keeping Short Accounts

Every generation needs someone who will stand in the place of the prophet and declare, "Thus saith the Lord." Someone who will unashamedly point out where we, as a people, have fallen short of God's standard.

The oft quoted, "A prophet is not without honor except in his own country," reveals how tough this job can be. Just read a few stories in the Old Testament, and you will gain a fresh appreciation for the man or woman with the courage to call a nation and her people to righteousness.

A prophet, however, faces temptation and challenges as all mortals do. If he yields to those forces, then he must repent quickly lest his guilt be manifested in even harsher judgment of others.

As the guilt gnaws at him, this exhorter will pound the table even harder while demanding integrity and purity from others. He will often exercise judgment by penalizing others for the very thing he is doing privately.

Everyone in leadership is called upon to pass judgment on issues of integrity. That is a fact that no leader can escape. The danger lies, however, in the leader's temptation to ignore his own guilt by treating others more harshly.

Unresolved guilt lowers our self-esteem, and out of that poor self-image a leader will use his influence or authority as a bloody pulpit.

How can we guard against this?

First, we must remember, as the apostle Paul said, "Such were some of you." There is no sin we could not commit save for the grace of God. Therefore, as leaders, we must evaluate others with a contrite heart that depends wholly on the Lord himself.

Secondly, keep a short account with God.

The human mind has no mechanism for handling guilt. Our mental hospitals are filled with people who have attempted to resolve guilt through abuse of drugs and alcohol.

Leaders, unfortunately, can often attempt to soothe their own conscience by judging others harshly. They abuse not only themselves but others in the process.

If we confess our sins daily, we receive the Lord's healing. This is not a confession for salvation, but rather an acknowledgment of our need for unhindered fellowship with the Father. Apart from His grace, sin and the judgment of others will be our constant companion.

5

Consensual Integrity

My dear friend Dan Johnson told me a story about a wise, seasoned minister who, with a friend, sat listening to the story being told by a young, visiting missionary. A question arose in the friend's mind and, reflecting, he asked the senior clergyman, "Do you believe what this young man is preaching?"

The response was quick, "*He* does."

It happens all the time. Somebody says something we know is not true, but we keep smiling and do nothing. It's too uncomfortable not to consent. We know better, but we hold back and give a foothold to the enemy of our souls.

We all must be brought to the truth.

Perhaps my greatest sin at PTL was consenting to some of the things that happened. It wasn't a deliberate decision. I just did nothing.

That doesn't mean I am not responsible. It just

means I should have known better. By not verbalizing my objections, I indicated I was not against what was going on at PTL. I kept quiet because I didn't want to overstep my bounds.

I know now that I should have lovingly but firmly asked, "What is going on?"

Consensual integrity happens at every level of life and society.

Husbands and wives live in adultery; teenagers con their parents; families pretend to be living the American dream — but because we're a part of it, we don't confront them with the truth. Institutions present a vague but dishonest assessment of their achievements; a church, college, or ministry fools its constituents, but we consent, hoping everything really is on the up and up.

We consent to their lies by the actions we do not take. We assent morally with our accord and unconsciously bring agreement to what is taking place. In our desire to be in harmony, we lose sight of reality.

Looking the Other Way

I admit it. I want to be liked. So do you. That's part of our humanity, and it's also part of our problem. Instead of focusing on ourselves, we need to simply, lovingly, and firmly move into the lives of those who are not living the truth. All of us must take the mantle and do it.

When we see some fallen person gasping for breath, we need to ask, "How can I respond to that person's need?" Do we just stand by and watch his expiration?

Do you know anyone who is losing or has lost

his integrity? Have you kindly and in a gentle but firm manner moved into his life to ask what is happening? If you don't, then you are consenting to his failure.

Leaders fall by the wayside, and some of us never notice. Why do we wait until it is too late to realize that someone has lost it all?

The Good Samaritan wasn't sent by a church, a denomination, or a committee. He was one man who stopped and cared.

When your heart tells you to do something — to reach out to someone who is failing — do it, and as quickly as possible. Don't consent to what is going on in their lives.

Our motives must be right, that's true. If our hearts are pure, we will not consent to things that are displeasing to our Heavenly Father.

Every group resolution or personal decision should be reviewed by each person who has an interest in that decision. For the sake of those deciding, we must not consent to what we know is not right. None of us are ever too big or mighty to be wrong.

We can no longer depend on the institutions of our society to speak to this problem of consensual integrity. It is now the responsibility of each individual.

It's easy to become too busy and insensitive to what our heart is saying. Besides, it takes courage to move into someone's life and speak in a loving, firm way to the problems he faces.

A common phrase among frequent churchgoers describes the exaggeration of a preacher. The phrase, "evangelistically speaking," is a euphemism for being less than honest.

How could a person, especially one in leadership, mislead people for so long without anyone knowing it? Do they simply fool everybody? Are they like the man who for years impersonated a doctor without getting caught because he was so competent?

While some may fall into this category of the professional con man, there is a far more subtle explanation: Others who know the truth simply go along; they acquiesce to what the group thinks.

Politicians applaud vigorously as their candidate promises the voters prosperity and peace, all the while knowing that he cannot deliver either.

Church leaders will listen to a mission report they know couldn't be accurate. They sit in silence, however, so as not to hurt the "faith" of others.

Advertisers make bold claims that the businessman knows cannot be wholly substantiated, but they tolerate it as part of the marketing effort. After all, who will really be harmed?

A president denies any knowledge of wrongdoing while his staff and closest aides know better, but in the interest of national security his remark goes unchallenged.

The problem, of course, is that people are harmed by such consensual integrity. The truth *does* make a difference regardless of who chooses to look the other way.

Who is Responsible?

No research carried out by the U.S. government impacts more Americans than the U.S. Census. It affects everything from the appropriation of tax money to voting districts.

Yet, the census, too, has become political. Congressmen know that integrity is breached. Nevertheless, it is accepted as simply "part of the process." Alvin Toffler summarizes the census problem:

> The ten year census questionnaire used in the United States must be approved by Congress. Says a senior census official: "Congress puts various pressures on us. We do a sample survey on farm finance. We've been directed by Congress not to collect that data because it might have been used to cut federal support for farmers." Companies in every industry also pressure the Census Bureau to ask, or to avoid asking, certain questions.[1]

The census has become not an instrument for collecting raw data, but rather politically correct data, regardless of veracity.

When those whom we trust to provide oversight and protection to the people choose to ignore the truth, the results can be devastating. The recent savings and loan scandal, which will cost the American taxpayer billions, has left people asking, "Who knew about these lapses in integrity, and why didn't they do something?"

As the cost of consensual integrity in the marketplace grows, so does the concern of people everywhere. In the closing weeks of 1991, a painful example came to light regarding the financial empire of the late Robert Maxwell.

Business Week reported on what appears to have happened:

> Robert Maxwell, 68, may have defrauded his two publicly traded companies of at least 1.4 billion, mainly by filching money from the companies' employee retirement funds, before his mysterious death at sea on November 5.[2]

How could this happen? Wasn't someone somewhere responsible for regulating the activity of a publicly traded company? Was Maxwell a master of fraud, or were others simply turning their head in their own best interest?

Unfortunately, the latter appears to be the case. *Business Week* went on to conclude,

> Maxwell would have been able to do little without the willing aid of his bankers . . . more likely, they were enticed by Maxwell's profligate borrowing, which generated handsome fees.[3]

As the blame is passed around, the little people bear the burden. While losing one's life savings is disastrous, the practice of consensual integrity can be even more costly. The fatal train derailment in Maryland caused by an operator who was under the influence of drugs provides a sad example. Airline pilots who fly too soon after drinking alcohol, while the rest of the crew pretend not to know, risk countless lives.

In prime time, a news program focused on several television evangelists who seem to be using less than honest fundraising practices. Was the media the first to uncover this information, or were fellow ministers aware of the deception all along?

Many people might cowardly back off from being a whistle blower by quoting the Lord's admonition that, "He who is without sin cast the first stone." But, remember, Jesus spoke to a crowd who had gathered for a one-sided lynching — not to a group sincerely investigating the truth.

To the contrary, the Scripture admonishes us that to choose not to do what is right is a sin of omission; and such failure is serious.

Guarding Against Temptation

Consensual integrity is tolerated for one reason — selfishness. And that reason hinges on two excuses: First, I don't want to get involved because it might cost me something. Secondly, I don't want to say anything because I might lose money or prestige from the very person I am confronting.

Either way we fall short because the Scriptures call for us to be men and women of integrity. The roar of the crowd must never entice us to go along with a lie or to hide from one. The price for ourselves and others is too great.

Consensual integrity is borne out of an individual's own bent for self-preservation. The cost of going against the popular consensus for the moment can appear frightening. No one understands this better than Jesus. His message of redemption ran counter to both the religious and secular culture of His day.

How can we guard against this strong temptation?

First, we must cultivate a passion for the Lord's will to be done rather than our own. It begins with a simple question: Given this same set of circumstances, what would Jesus do?

That question, made popular in Charles Sheldon's classic book, *In His Steps,*[4] carries great weight. By asking it before you act, and by searching the Scripture for the answer, you will more often than not make the right decision.

The apostle Paul warned us that our battle would not be of the flesh but of the spirit. Ultimately, we resist the lure of consensual integrity not by our own strength but by the power of the Holy Spirit.

Remember Peter's failure on the night Jesus was arrested when he went along with the rest of the crowd and denied knowing the Lord? Yet, in Acts 4, Peter stood before the council and, under threat of his life, proclaimed Jesus as Lord.

What happened? What made the difference? The answer is found back in Acts when the passage reveals, "Then Peter filled with the Holy Ghost spoke" (Acts 4:8).

Ultimately our dependency, day by day, and moment by moment, upon the Holy Spirit is our only sure defense against consensual integrity. As we take the sinner's place, He empowers us to serve Him — faithfully!

The Big Picture

Painful and ugly. That's how I describe the

loss of my integrity. I take no pride in having learned the lessons I've shared with you. But I do believe God took my imprisonment and turned it around for good in my life.

Several days after I entered prison, a fellow inmate asked me to accompany him on a walk. He said he had something important to tell me.

"Do you know who I am?" he asked me.

"I'm not quite sure," I responded, somewhat intimidated, "but your name is Joe LaMotta, isn't it?"

As the son of the legend, Jake LaMotta — a former boxing champion called "the raging bull" — Joe had made a reputation for himself in the prison.

"Yes, it is," he replied.

Then Joe looked me straight in the eye. "When you came into the camp, I didn't think I was going to like you," he said, "but I've changed my mind in the last few days. You have been polite to me."

He paused for a moment then added, "There's something you need to know."

I held my breath, waiting for what this brute of a man would say. "You be strong," he almost commanded. "God sent you here!"

Although I wasn't looking for a message about how God felt about my being in prison, I paid attention when this burly inmate spoke. Hardly anyone ever disagreed with Joe LaMotta and neither did I. I believed him.

That message, coming from a most unlikely source, however, confirmed to me something I had already been sensing in my spirit: God was still in control.

Somehow I knew that even through this experience, the Master of the universe still loved me and was orchestrating every step along the way. That thought gave me courage to see beyond my pain to the bigger picture God had in mind.

That's why I approached the writing of this book with such solemnity. I do not take it lightly that God permitted me to go through the experiences of the past few years. My sole purpose is to be faithful to Him.

Let me leave you with four principles that, I hope, will help keep your integrity intact:

First, integrity involves our relationship to one another and our relationship to God.

Some of us breech our integrity in a more refined way than others and some not as frequently. Many people live right up to the dividing line of integrity, teetering on the fence or leaning across the line — just "living on the edge."

But anyone who has ever sinned is a part of the integrity problem. This is not a question of you or me. It is *us!* Let's ask ourselves: Am I dishonest? Am I prone *not* to tell the truth about myself and others? Am I denying what I know to be true?

Let's have the courage to place our hearts under the microscope and discover how integrity works in each of us. It's time to face the tough truth.

Second, anyone can lose his integrity. No one is immune.

It doesn't matter how you were raised, where you live, what church you attend, or even what you believe. Without constant diligence to the little things in life, your integrity can quickly slip through your hands.

Guard your integrity with mutual account-ability to your family and friends. When you sin, admit it and keep short, daily accounts with the Lord. Seek the help of the Holy Spirit, and God will "make your paths straight."

Third, integrity involves the wholeness of our inner person — our heart, mind, and will.

Integrity simply means *singleness:* singleness of our purpose, singleness of our will, singleness of our heart. When our integrity is intact, nothing divides the wholeness of who we are and what we are about.

Dr. Arthur Parsons, the man who helped me more than any other Christian leader, said to me on one occasion, "To be honest, you have to be honest."

Profound? Yes, if you are seeking to be a person of integrity.

Fourth, integrity can be regained.

The psalmist David did some very foolish and sinful things, but interestingly, God said, "This is a man after my own heart!" Why?

David said, "Let integrity and uprightness preserve me, I wait on thee!" Spoken by the man who went to bed with Bathsheba and fathered two illegitimate children; the adulterer who had Uriah killed talked about integrity.

God didn't say that David was always righteous. God didn't say that David was always spiritually correct. God *did* say that he was a man after His own heart.

There is hope after failure! There is peace and joy after dying to yourself. We must be willing to admit our mistakes, clean up our duplicity, and live again.

6

Failure v. *Success*

It's tough to admit, but one day I had to look myself in the mirror and say, "Richard Dortch, you failed. You failed God; you failed your fellow man; you failed your family; you failed yourself."

That admission wrenched my soul, and I grieved for the man I thought I had been. Now stripped naked before Almighty God and the world, I saw myself for what I was — a failure.

Why did I fail?

I have asked myself that question many times.

Did the enemy of my soul overpower me and take me prisoner? Did someone strike me down from behind in the dark? Did I purposely set out to commit a crime?

I knew in my heart that I and the other PTL executives had not intended to defraud the public or bring hurt to people that we love. How then did I get to this place in my life?

As I have walked through my own failures, I'm convinced that my problem was not *what I did*

— but *what I failed to do.*

All my life I had believed if I was simply pious and did no wrong, everything would be all right. Since then I have learned it is just as dangerous and treacherous *not* to do something as it is to be involved in aggressive sin.

We often think that we maintain our holiness by what we do *not* do, instead of by what we *do.* Obviously, there are certain sins that are damaging and damning. But, when we know to do good and do not do it, that also is sin.

The Greatest Man who ever lived taught us that truth again and again — sometimes in unusual and dramatic ways.

> Now in the morning, when He returned to the city, He became hungry. And seeing a lone fig tree by the road, He came to it, and found nothing on it except leaves only; and He said to it, "No longer shall there ever be any fruit from you." And at once the fig tree withered (Matt. 21:18-19).

What was wrong with the fig tree that Jesus cursed? Why did He command that it dry up and die? Was it spewing forth poison? Did its branches reach out to prick and wound? No. It had only one fault. It produced nothing but leaves. The fig tree had failed to do what it had been created to do — produce fruit.

Can that same charge be leveled against many of us? Have we failed to do our duty? Do our personal lives produce no fruit? Have we neglected certain situations and people when we should have become involved?

What about the five foolish virgins who brought along no extra oil for their lamps? They arrived on time; they brought their lamps; they were willing to wait for the bridegroom. They did all the right things. But they had no oil for their lamps. For that reason, the bridegroom said, "Truly I say to you, I do not know you."

Why such a harsh indictment? They had failed in their duty.

Why Do We Fail?

When we fail, it is usually not the result of ignorance. Most of us know what we are supposed to do and the importance of why we should do it. When it comes to moral or spiritual failure, as Christians, we cannot plead ignorance.

More knowledge won't change the facts, either; we are capable of discerning right from wrong. What we need is the will to live up to what we already know. Failure results because we are unwilling to follow through on what we know to be right.

When situations arise that aren't proper, we fail by not acting to correct them. We ignore the tugging on our hearts. Instead of affirming the proper action, we weigh the pros and cons and then sit idly by while problems continue and circumstances deteriorate.

How *should* we respond?

We must do what Jesus would have done in that situation. In a loving and kind way, we should move into the lives of people and declare what we know to be right.

"In all thy ways acknowledge Him, and He shall direct thy paths" (Prov. 3:6).

I cannot plead ignorance nor can I blame my failures on lack of ability. If that were true, I would never have been hired as an executive at PTL.

Maybe I failed because I was lazy. But looking back, I know that's not the case either. In fact, I have always given above and beyond the call of duty in every position I have held.

If I didn't fail because of ignorance, inability, or idleness, what caused my downfall? I think I know.

I was *too busy*. I cannot deny it.

The secondary so absorbed us at PTL that we neglected the primary. We had so much that was good that it robbed us of the privilege of doing our best.

I was like the prodigal son starving in the far country.

> And he went and attached himself to one of the citizens of that country, and he sent him into his fields to feed swine. And he was longing to fill his stomach with the pods that the swine were eating, and no one was giving anything to him. But when he came to his senses, he said, "How many of my father's hired men have more than enough bread, but I am dying here with hunger!" (Luke 15:15-16).

He definitely had a problem, but it was not

that he was in a hog pen. If he'd been in a king's palace, he would still have been a failure. Why? Because he was missing out on the best God had for him — the privilege of being in his father's house.

The sin we should fear the most is not the sin of vicious wrongdoing; it is the sin of choosing second best. That's what the prodigal son did, and that's where we usually fail God.

If we spend most of our time doing trivial things, we rob ourselves of doing something better. Much of our time is spent on activities and procedures that are good, perhaps, but not the best.

At PTL we were often engaged in great, stressful, straining trivialities. While not sinister or malicious, these secondary priorities so absorbed us that we didn't have time left to do what God had called us to do. We were involved in a thousand and one decent and wonderful programs and ministries; but while we were busy here and there, something of God slipped out of our lives. Our "busyness" kept us so preoccupied that we didn't have a keen interest in simply "knowing God," which should be every Christian's highest goal.

I learned a painful lesson: To maintain integrity I must put first things first.

Listen to the voice of the Greatest Man who ever lived. This is His message:

> But seek ye first the kingdom of God, and his righteousness; and all these things shall be added unto you (Matt. 6:33).

That verse pounded in my spirit from the day the bubble burst and the castle crumbled. When we fail to seek the Kingdom first — even though the task be noble and the toil hard — we will not taste in the end the joy of victory we so desperately sought.

When Dreams Turn to Ashes

After I was removed from my position at PTL and learned that I faced criminal charges, I wondered over and over, "Why did this happen to me?"

I was disillusioned — about life, about people, and about myself.

In our domain of television, I had lived a fairy tale existence. For years I had been writing the script for triumphs, but I had left out the scenes on testings.

I had known trials before; sickness, grief, and weariness were not strangers to me. But now I faced failure, financial pressure, desertion by friends, closed doors.

Like a child I had lived in innocence for a long time, but I quickly came into an age of accountability and things were never the same again. My "Alice in Wonderland" world dissipated in a few days, and I was awakened from my dreams. It was time for me to grow up.

I had never deserved the positions, the accolades, and the recognition that came my way. God helped me to understand that maybe I didn't "deserve" what I was getting from the press, the people, or the courts either. But I was thrown into the school of life, and I had lessons to learn. The stern realities of living through the indictment, the court appearance, and, finally, prison were part of God's course in maturity. I knew they would make me the person God wanted me to be — if I would let them.

In desperation, I began to search for answers.

Often the biblical character, Joseph, came to my mind. Behind bars, all his childhood dreams seemed to mock him. I knew how he felt.

> And Joseph's master took him, and put him into the prison, a place where the king's prisoners were bound: and he was there in the prison (Gen. 39:20).

During the dark hours of prison life, I had to come to grips with the things I had learned during the daylight of blessing. Would they work in the blackness?

I soon learned I would survive, and in doing so I would grow stronger. Although I certainly hadn't planned for the events of my life to work out this way, when I look back, I wouldn't want to change a thing. I wouldn't have it any other way.

The sorrows made me search further until I made new discoveries of faith that deepened my life and ministry.

Permit me to share them with you.

The God of the Mountains

In the months after my indictment and conviction, the great Bible stories I had learned as a child became alive to me. One, in particular, underscored a new truth: God is Lord not only of the mountain top experiences but also of the valleys.

When Ahab was king of Israel, God had poured out blessings upon His people in a wonderful way. Divine protection surrounded the northern kingdom of Israel, and their enemies were defeated on the battlefields.

One of Israel's victories was so wonderful that no explanation could possibly be given, other than "the might and the power of the Lord." Hopelessly outnumbered, the children of Israel had arrayed themselves in battle formation against the Syrians.

The fight took place on top of the mountains; the Syrians were defeated. It seemed the host of heaven had been fighting on the side of the people of the Lord.

The northern country was hilly and mountainous, and many of their cities were built high up on the mountain tops. Woven like a thread through Israel's customs, culture, and religious literature was the story of the mountains and the glory of the hills. They were a hill people, while the Syrians were children of the plains.

Perhaps Ben-hadad considered this fact.

He couldn't understand defeat and wondered, How could such a little army defeat a force as large as his? Knowing that the God of Israel had brought about the victory, the king reached a conclusion: God was a God of the mountains and not a God of the valleys.

Ben-hadad decided to go to battle once again.

The bugle call sounded throughout the Syrian countryside, summoning an army exactly the size of the one that had been defeated. The king insisted on man for man, horse for horse, and chariot for chariot. He must have felt sure of his ground.

The day of battle came. On one side were the armies of Syria — a tremendous group of soldiers assembled under Ben-hadad. Confidence filled the air. They felt certain of victory. The Syrian king would prove to the whole world that the God of Israel might be the God of the mountain top, but He was certainly not the God of the valleys.

On the other side of the valley, the army of Israel gathered. In comparison to the size of the Syrian army, King Ahab's men looked like two small herds of goats.

> Then a man of God came near and spoke to the king of Israel and said, "Thus says the Lord, 'Because the Syrians have said, "The LORD is a god of the mountains, but He is not a god of the valleys"; therefore I will give all this great multitude into your hand, and you shall know that I am the LORD'" (1 Kings 20:28).

When the battle was over, Israel had killed 100,000 Syrian soldiers, leaving Ben-hadad's army broken and defeated. Thousands of their remaining soldiers fled in dismay, taking refuge beneath the city wall. Further disaster awaited them there as the wall fell and crumbled upon them. Thousands perished at the hand of the Lord.

God had proven that He was not only the God of the mountains, but He was also the God of the valleys.

I had known God to be the God of the mountains. Most of my life had been spent on the peaks, and I was quick to praise God for the victories. It was great to shout for joy, glorying in the fact that my head was above the clouds. Most of my testimonies and sermons had been about the mountain top experiences.

During those rare visits in the valley, however, I forgot to praise God. Instead, I looked with envious eyes at the people who had come out of the valley to the mountains peaks of victory.

That changed when the valley became my dwelling place for five years.

I look back and see that the circumstances at which I initially cringed proved to hold the richest and sweetest lessons of life. The trials that beset me became a benediction in disguise. I was developing strength by testing, and I knew that my character and integrity would be attained by overcoming in the valley.

The Valley of Blessing

Valleys are actually much safer than mountains. In our heartaches and trials, the danger of forgetting God is far less than when we are living beneath the cloudless sky on the pinnacles of success.

It was in the dark valley of defeat that I wept tears of sorrow and felt the need of Jesus. Difficulties forced me to my knees, and I longed for strength and an arm that would not fail me.

In the past, I had depended on others to keep things going. Now when the winds of adversity were striking and the hurricanes of life were whirling around me, I looked to "the Rock that was higher than I."

Often my wife and I, in discussing our trials, would say, "It feels like there has been a death in the family." Indeed, we seemed to be standing beside an open grave. With anticipation, I kept waiting for the angels to sing an anthem of resurrection, but they were long in coming.

I was lonely and longed for companionship, the kind the disciples found on the road to Emmaus. And like them, I made many new discoveries about the risen Saviour.

There is another danger on the mountain top. It's easy to backslide when we're going to church and doing the Lord's work. In the place of seeming safety, our relationship to God borders on the casual. Integrity can be easily lost when we are most secure.

Jesus' mother lost Him in the house of worship, and thousands of us have lost Him in the same place. We are far more likely to ignore Jesus when we're on the mountain than when we are in the valley.

At times we can skip along the pathway with a spring in our step and a song in our heart. There isn't a cloud in the sky. God's blessings become commonplace, and we neglect the altars in our hearts because there's no special need to pray.

In the valley, however — with its heartaches, trials, tears, and sorrows — prayer never escapes our hearts or lips. We fear moving away from the Saviour's side for even a moment.

Growth takes place in the valleys far more than when we are at ease on the mountain top. I learned very little while I riding high, both as a well-known denominational executive and, later, as a TV personality. In ruin and failure, however, the lessons of the Bible became real.

We learn very little from our successes; we learn much more from our failures.

7

Why Do Trials Come?

When everything was going wrong in my life, I blamed the media, my detractors, those who despised me, and sometimes my friends for my problems. I often told those who would listen, "Certainly the enemy of our souls is after me."

It must have been a monotonous, repetitious thing that I asserted — that the devil was testing me and bringing these trials to my life.

When I felt happy, I would say it was the Lord's goodness; when I felt pain, I said it was the devil. I was confident that all my afflictions came from the pit.

Today I'm inclined to give less credit to the adversary of our souls. I do not like him, and he does not like me; but during these troubled times, my eyes have been opened to a greater truth.

Foolish whimpering about testings and trials coming from Satan has stopped. Why? Because I am absolutely convinced that the vast majority of my trials were permitted by the Lord.

Why would our heavenly Father, who loves us and protects us, allow His children to endure trials and suffering?

I believe the difficulties and testings in our lives are sent by the Lord to strengthen us in faith and to make us grow in grace. Why would there be grace unless it was needed? Why would there be strength unless it was required? Why would there be power unless there was some victory to be won?

The apostle Paul discovered this secret. How many times in his letters did he rejoice and glory in his victories? I cannot find even one. Every time Paul's heart fills with praise and words of gratitude, it comes as a result of his trials and testings.

Did he not rejoice in his infirmities? Did he not glory in a cross? Did he not have praise for his afflictions? Had he not arrived at the conclusion that these were the things that were working out for him a far more exceeding glory? The apostle Paul came to a place in his experience where he knew that his trials and testings were far more important than his victories.

We must learn, like Paul, to rejoice in our infirmities.

The secret of leaning hard on God is to get into the circumstance where He's the only One holding you up. You can only know of God's companionship when He has stood beside you through heartache and sorrow.

Why does He permit the trials and the testings? To make us better, of course. To make us nobler, sweeter, and to illustrate — in a way we'll never forget — that we are totally dependent upon Him.

Dormant faith will never make an impression, but active, alive faith will bring honor and glory to the One who deserves it. We need God, both on the mountain top and in the valley. But, we are more likely to sense our need of Him in the valley experiences of life.

We say we believe that "all things work together for good to them that love God" (Rom. 8:28). Then as soon as some of the "all things" happen, we begin to whimper and cry and say that the devil is attacking us. That is not consistent.

If "the steps of a good person are ordered by the Lord" (Ps. 37:23), who are we to question where He takes us? We must come to the place where we sincerely believe that everything— both the good and bad — does not happen by chance.

Songs in the Night

When we're not blaming the devil, we're imagining that the heartache we've come through was God's punishment for our shortcomings. I don't believe so. God is not trying to get even with us by taking us into the valleys of life. He loves us too much for that.

For me, the tears that fell and the sorrows that beset me were not punitive, they were remedial. If they were punitive, then I would be atoning for my own wrongs. That could never be.

Our Saviour atoned for my sins — and yours — by what He suffered on the cross.

I cannot say that God was punishing me, but He was trying to get my attention.

His chastisements are for our own good.

> He disciplines us for your good,
> that we may share His holiness. All
> discipline for the moment seems not to
> be joyful, but sorrowful; yet to those
> who have been trained by it, afterwards
> it yields the peaceful fruit of righteous-
> ness (Heb. 12:11).

When we view God's discipline in light of the future, we can understand that hidden somewhere in them is His good and ultimate purpose for us.

The burden I bear today — the heartache and sorrow that is mine — will prove to be a blessing and bring light to my tomorrows. The beauty of godly character shines all the more brightly against the dark background of difficulty and trial.

It was in the Philippian jail that Paul and Silas went on record for singing hallelujahs. After being thrown into the inner prison and their feet fastened in stocks, "about midnight Paul and Silas were praying and singing hymns of praise to God, and the prisoners were listening to them" (Acts 16:25).

The songs that sound the sweetest are the ones that ring through the darkness of the night. I know this to be true: the song in the night is sweeter by far than the song in the day.

Put to the Test

God took Abraham into the valley.

As he trudged across the plains toward Mount Moriah carrying a bundle of sticks, a young boy walked beside him.

"Daddy, where is the sacrifice?" Issac asks. "We have wood for the fire, but what are we going to offer as the sacrifice when we get there?"

Abraham swallows hard against the tightness in his throat. Anguished lines wrinkle his grief-stricken face as he remembers the words of his God:

> "Take now your son, your only son, whom you love, Issac, and go to the land of Moriah; and offer him there as a burnt offering on one of the mountains of which I will tell you" (Gen. 22:2).

What a valley experience that was! What a trial and testing for this old man !

But how can you — or God, for that matter — know how strong faith is unless it's put to the test? How can you know how much you trust the Lord until you are tried and tested?

If we could have been there and joined Abraham in the midst of the valley, he would probably have said, "This is the hardest thing I've ever done in my life. I am perplexed and bewildered. I cannot understand, but I know my confidence and trust are in the Lord."

Through the deep, dark valley on his way to Mount Moriah, Abraham must have felt the shadows engulfing him like death's jaws.

But deliverance came on the mountain! How wonderfully Abraham was brought through that experience. Victory came out of defeat!

> And Abraham stretched out his hand, and took the knife to slay his son. But the angel of the LORD called to him

from heaven, and said, "Abraham, Abraham!" And he said, "Here I am."

And he said, "Do not stretch out your hand against the lad, and do nothing to him; for now I know that you fear God, since you have not withheld your son, your only son, from Me."

Then Abraham raised his eyes and looked, and behold, behind him a ram caught in the thicket by his horns; and Abraham went and took the ram, and offered him up for a burnt offering in the place of his son.

And Abraham called the name of that place, The LORD Will Provide, as it is said to this day, "In the mount of the Lord it will be provided" (Gen. 22:10-14).

The story of Abraham's faith was so glorious and beautiful that angels must have looked at it and wondered. Even today us mortals stand in contemplation.

Down the mountainside came Abraham and his boy. The old man's heart, filled with God's presence and glory, overflowed. His joy was more wonderful than words could tell.

Into the Sunlight

Remember, the thing that seems grievous to you today will shine like a jewel in the sunlight of another morning.

Our God is truly the God of the mountains, but He is also the God of the valleys. I know because I have walked through them. Yes, He is the Lord of the mountains and the valleys.

There is more blessing in the battle than in the victory that follows it.

When the trials of life hurt us, we can rest in the sublime consciousness of God's abiding presence, His never-failing care, and His undying love. Then the light will shine in the darkness, and faith will sing in the night, and you will know the truth of pure integrity. Wholeness has come.

In days to come, when you're in the midst of battles, as I have been, I pray that the Holy Spirit will reach into the chambers of your memory and hold before your eyes the scenes I've shared with you.

The God whom you love and adore is the God of your mountains. But the richer and sweeter lessons in life will be learned when you lift your tear-stained eyes heavenward and raise your heart toward the skies and declare — He is the God of the valleys, too.

8

Loving Yourself

Most of us have read and re-read the phrase from the Gospel according to St. Matthew, "Thou shalt love thy neighbor as thyself" (19:19). We repeat the words piously in church, and we invoke the need to be concerned about others.

Jesus, however, also makes it clear in that verse you are to love yourself! He readily accepted self-love and did not rebuke it.

How you love yourself reveals how you will love your family, associates, and neighbors.

Loving yourself brings into focus your uniqueness. Think of it: millions of souls have never been — and will never again be — duplicated exactly. You are an original, fashioned precisely the way God designed you.

Because I have learned some valuable lessons in life and want to flee from power and all of its accompaniments, I am having to re-learn the art of loving myself as God desires. Let me share some principles I have gleaned about loving myself as the person that I am.

1. Learn to establish your presence.

It's possible to do this without brashness or conceit when we know God has a specific plan for our lives.

The apostle Paul is a good example. When the apostle arrived on the scene, people knew that a man who walked with God was in their presence. Yet he did so by being himself with his security firm in Christ.

As a young man, I had the privilege of having lunch with Ernest S. Williams, a revered man who had been the top executive and spiritual leader of our denomination for more than two decades. I was struck with awe at this ninety-year-old minister. For me he seemed to be the father of our church.

During our meal, I tried to ask him some questions that were important to me. "What are your priorities in life? What was important to you years before that is no longer important today?" I wanted to learn from him.

Finally, after several questions, this righteous man stopped his eating, looked directly into my eyes, and said, "Just do it like I did, and you'll end up all right."

There was more truth in that statement than I realized at the time.

It was the same kind of wise confidence that led Paul to write, "Follow me as I follow Christ." He wasn't attempting to push himself forward, he was just being himself.

2. Believe you are God's person.

If you have been called to a task, the Lord must know that you are capable. Do it with gusto, not with a weary feeling of duty! If you know God has called and assigned you to a particular job, you can be content without trying to force your way up the ladder.

I became a Christian as a boy. When Oral Roberts preached in my home church in Granite City, Illinois, I walked forward and knelt at an altar. For me it was a symbol of surrender, of giving my life to Christ. I had only one desire: to be a Christian.

As I began to walk with the Lord, I prayed, read my Bible, and participated in the activities of the church. After joining the youth program, I wanted to become a leader in the group. Then, as a young man, I thought it would be wonderful if I could be trained as a pastor. After attending college, I was offered my first pastorate.

Then I prayed, "Lord, if I just had the opportunity to be a leader of a group of churches. . . ." Then I became an area leader.

Then I wanted to be a missionary. While serving in Belgium, I hoped to be appointed an officer over an area of our denomination in Europe, and I was.

I wanted to be president of a Bible school, and I was.

That was not sufficient, and I said, "Lord, if I could be a person of some authority on the state level to manage the business affairs of our denomination. . . ." Then that opportunity came. But it was not enough.

I said, "Lord, if I could have the power to be the state superintendent as a bishop in the church." And I was.

"Oh, God, that I would be a leader on the national level of our church." And I was.

And on and on it went until God gave me the opportunity to touch not only my community and my state but the world through the ministry of PTL. Until it all came crashing down.

The day came when I bumped into God and came back to the prayer I prayed as a young person: "Oh, God, that I could just be a Christian." I wanted nothing more!

The point of this is what the prophet said: "All is vanity and vexation of spirit." After you've got it all, what have you? Nothing. That's the bottom line.

Too often we move away from the simplicity that is in Christ to things that are totally unrelated to the spiritual part of our lives.

There are more of us who are power seekers on power drives than we care to admit.

3. Know that God's kind of success is available to those who desire His best!

Whether it is winning a contract, teaching a class, a notable achievement, a promotion, or giving a speech, we must realize our full potential. Don't accept less!

Success must be linked to effectiveness. That is the real measure of success — that we are doing our job successfully but also effectively. To get the most out of what we do, we must want to do it and be willing to pay the price to achieve the best.

4. Contribute something!

View yourself as being able to do something

for people, for the Kingdom, or for the company where you work. Have a servant's heart.

Not long ago, a friend came to me and said, "You will always be a leader to me, whether or not you hold any office."

"Why is that?" I asked him.

"Because when you were my bishop and I was under your leadership, we knew you loved us." His words meant a great deal to me.

I had considered myself a mentor, a leader, a counselor, a friend to these dear people — not because of my official title or elected position — but because of the relationships that had been formed. As a result, my love was unquestioned.

Because of the associations I had developed with people over the years, I received letters from church officers — while I was in prison — asking for my recommendation for men being considered as pastoral candidates.

Although I have admitted many of my faults that led to my downfall, I can honestly say that when I held positions of power in the church, I did not operate as a pompous leader.

5. Accept full responsibility for being what you are.

Don't alibi! We all have problems in our backgrounds, hurts in our pasts, and "skeletons in our closets," but our Lord is the Master Forgiver and Healer of our hurts. We cannot wallow in the past forever!

6. Strive for the best, but don't be a hypocrite!
Learn from those around you, but don't try to

imitate them. Be yourself as you are spiritually directed.

Early in my ministry, my beloved Aunt Marie kept me on course by listening to me and leveling with me. Long ago, after I took my first pastorate, I invited her to come and teach a series of messages in the church I was pastoring.

I was thrilled to offer such a great opportunity to my aunt, but most of all I was glad she would see me in action! I put on quite a show when she arrived, leading the people in worship and waxing eloquent.

When the service was over, and I knew I had "wowed" both the church and my visitor, we sat down for a snack. Aunt Marie looked across the table and said, "Richard, what's your problem?"

"Problem?"

"I'll tell you," she continued. "You're living closer to the people than you are to God."

I was stunned! But instantly I knew she was right. She touched my soul with her candid words: "When you live close to God, He rubs off on you. It shows up in your conversation and in everything you do. But when you live closer to your people, you soon begin reflecting their value system."

"What should I do?"

"You must walk close enough to God," she counseled, "that these people can see Him in you. Then they will want more of Him."

7. Study people who are leaders and learn from them.

Read the great biographies about men and women who were effective leaders — achievers who kept a balanced view of themselves. Study the things that people have done, what they said, what they wrote. Open your mind to a dimension of their thinking.

As yourself questions like: What does Billy Graham teach about God's love and mercy? What kind of life does he lead?

Study the life of Mother Teresa. You'll learn what it means to serve others who can give you nothing in return.

Mark and Hulda Buntain, missionaries to India, are two of my personal heroes. For nearly half a century, they have given their lives totally to God and the people of Calcutta. Even since Mark's death, Hulda has carried on the work of feeding and educating the needy children of Calcutta.

8. Develop a passion for excellence.

Most people are followers, not leaders. And few people become great leaders.

Doug Kingsritter played for a championship football team in high school and college and was an All American tight end. He later played in the National Football League. After being with the Minnesota Vikings and several Super Bowl teams, he was asked, "What's the difference between the coaching in high school, college, and the professionals?"

He thought a moment then replied, "The coaches in high school and college probably know as much, but Coach Bud Grant sees *everything* that happens when the Vikings are playing. He never misses a thing."

A great leader single-mindedly focuses on the

area of his concern and becomes an expert through study, discipline, and experience.

9. Be disciplined — in body, soul, and spirit.
We must bring ourselves to the discipline of denying ourselves. Let us do without things we hold dear to us.

Take care of your body. Work hard, sleep well, and eat what you need, not what you want. Before you eat, ask yourself, Is this what I need, or is it what I want.

Exercise! No one else can do it for you.

Life must be disciplined. How we live and feel tells much about how we discipline ourselves. I have had to come face to face with this issue.

Keep asking yourself, Why am I doing this? I will be judged eternally for all things. We must nurture our souls. Be quiet. Listen to your heart. Don't close it down. Do what is right! Tell the truth. Live in private like you do in public. Let your soul feed on things that are wholesome.

Keep a good attitude! Stay sweet! Don't fight, you will never win! Rest in God! Maintain a quiet and gentle spirit.

Keep your mind under discipline. What is going on in your mind? Remember, evil begins in the imagination. Keep your mind pure. Evil may drive by your mind, but don't give it a parking place.

10. Keep it simple.
Have a livable lifestyle. Don't compete with your neighbors. Don't get in debt beyond your ability to pay it back comfortably. Share with oth-

ers God's goodness to you!

Be content with what God has given you. He knows how much you can handle.

Pray this prayer: "O Lord, . . . Keep falsehood and lies far from me; give me neither poverty nor riches, but give me only my daily bread. Otherwise, I may have too much and disown you and say, 'Who is the Lord?'" (Prov. 30:7-9).

King Solomon knew the danger of having too much money, but like many others, he failed to follow his own advice.

11. Don't be a prima donna and don't be pompous.

We need to remove the elitist spirit out of our hearts.

Let's put our telephone numbers back in the directory. Let us be disturbed during our meals. During our days off, let the calls come. Let us be awakened in the middle of the night for hurting, needy people. Let us be needed in our moments of rest by sobbing souls yearning to speak to us.

12. Tell the truth, only and always!

When you deceive, you are the most deceived.

There is a vast difference between a confidence and a secret. A secret is something known only to us. A confidence is something we share in confidence with a confidential relationship. It will never be told.

If you don't have the ability to hold a confidence, you shouldn't make others believe you can be trusted. People ask, "Will you keep this a secret? Can I talk to you in confidence?"

If you are not going to do that, don't lie. Be honest and say, "No, I can't do it."

13. Don't talk about yourself all the time.

Be interested in others! Your projects and plans are very important, but so are those of other people! Learn to listen.

All the great men I have known were genuinely interested in others. Those who only spoke of themselves, however, often failed.

14. Don't quit!

It is a sin to do less than your best. Keep at a task until it is finished. Never, never, never give up. You will win, probably because you endured. Stick to the job.

Do not accept defeat easily. Keep moving forward. Your Creator will help you to create answers to your problems and needs. God's creative genius is yours for the asking.

Unfortunately, any feelings of unworthiness you may have are often compounded when problems arise. You need to learn how to meet life's turbulence and ups and downs.

Though He was perfection incarnate, our Lord faced a less than perfect world. The apostle Paul, a man of human frailty like ourselves, also met many triumphs and tragedies. None of us are exempt from the difficulties and problems of life.

9

Finding Yourself

After ten months of incarceration in federal prison, my health began to fail. At first the prison doctors were treating me for a hernia. Then, during an examination before the surgery, one of the attending physicians asked, "Why are your ankles so swollen?"

I said, "I don't know."

"We need to do a CAT scan," he stated.

Three days after the hernia surgery, they did the scan and the same doctor came back to my bedside to report the results. "You know, I'm almost positive that you have cancer," he said as gently as possible. "Tomorrow I want to send you downtown and get an MRI."

The next day after the MRI, he returned to say, "I'm very sorry to tell you that you do have cancer. It's life threatening, and we'll have to take your kidney out."

A few days later, I was back in surgery.

After the operation, recovery came slowly,

and I walked with a cane for over six months.

In the middle of the Florida summer, out in the prison yard, I wore an overcoat because I was always cold. It seemed I was getting well, but my body hadn't been notified.

One day, a few months before I knew I would be released from prison, I was talking with another inmate, Ed Taylor, a true brother in Christ. "Ed," I said, "I've got to write David Wilkerson and tell him I am sorry."

"Why?" he asked.

"I've got to make things right. When I had begged him to come to PTL, we didn't have an argument, but I could sense there was tension between us. I knew he could not find a release in his own spirit to come to PTL, but I kept insisting. I realize now that I had a contentious spirit. My pleading and urging were not being responded to, and I was used to having my way. I want to be forgiven for my attitude that day when he called and warned me about the pending judgment coming upon PTL."

Ed looked at me for a moment, then said, "Yes, it would be good for you to write to him and clear the air."

Five days passed, and I had not yet written to pastor wilkerson. When I went to the post office that day, the officer called my name and handed me a letter,

When I looked at the return address, I read: David Wilkerson, Pastor Christ Church, Times Square, New York City.

My heart nearly stopped, and I thought, I sure hope he hasn't heard from the Lord again. Oh, I don't need this. Not another word from the Lord. Not here; not now. I don't think I can take another rebuke.

Too afraid to open the envelope in the mail room, I went back to my dormitory. It was time for the evening meal. As 163 men filed out to go to eat, I stayed alone in my modular cube.

I sat on my cot, staring at the envelope in my hand. I had already been thrown out of my denomination. It was my fault, not theirs. Prison had been easy compared to being rejected by my brothers and sisters in Christ. In my weakened condition, I felt I couldn't bear up under more rejection.

In the 22 inches from the side of the wall to the bed, I got down on my knees and began to pray. "Lord, you have helped me to walk through everything that has happened, and I still have a kind, sweet spirit. Lord, I don't want to allow bitterness and rebellion into my heart. I want to come through this with victory. So, Lord, when I open this letter and read whatever this prophet of God has to say, help me to receive it as a word from You. Help me to accept it with the right spirit."

God Loves! God Forgives!

I got up from my knees, sat on the cot, and opened the letter.

The first words I read were, "Brother Dortch, I love you."

I sighed, overwhelmed with a sense of relief. I sensed the love that Brother David Wilkerson was showing as the love of Christ. The joy, the peace, and the exhilaration of knowing that somebody cared about me flooded my soul.

Then I read the next words: "I have a word from the Lord." By then, the fear had lifted, and I knew God was going to speak to me.

I listen to brother David's words. He told me that he knew what I would do when I got out of prision. You are going to try to make up to God for what took place. I know you are sorry and that you want to do what is right.

I smiled to myself, realizing God knew the inner secrets of my heart.

I read on.

"God will restore all the years the canker worm has eaten. When you are released, He's going to give you such an abounding harvest that all shall be made up to you. It will be as if nothing has been lost. . . . You need not make up anything for Him — He will make it up to you. What a tender, loving Father we serve."

I could hard believe my eyes. I read it again to be sure. "He wants to make it up to you!"

I came apart; I wept. There was a loving, forgiving Saviour. I knew it! I had preached it for years, but now someone was whispering it to me, "We have a loving heavenly Father."

Brushing the tears from my eyes, I continued to read — now with great excitement at receiving any further words the Lord had for me.

". . . The Spirit of God is upon you — your call is intact — and your reputation shall be restored."

The tears fell uncontrollably from my eyes, dotting the page and smearing the ink. I pulled back not wanting anything to mar the precious words I held in my hand.

". . . As you give Him all and pursue Him with

all your heart, you will come forth without even the smell of smoke upon you as did the Hebrew children out of the furnace."

As I neared the end of the letter, Brother David Wilkerson wrote, ". . . You are well remembered and beloved by many of us. We anxiously await the time when we can see you face to face and have you share with our body how He sustained you and taught you so much of Himself. We love you."

Suddenly, it hit me. God had forgiven me for my pride, my arrogance, my haughty spirit, and now He wanted to do something beautiful in my life. As far as the east is from the west, so far has He removed our transgressions from us. I realized there is nothing I could ever do to stop God from loving me.

I threw my head back and shouted praises to God within my heart and soul. As my spirit rejoiced, I began to sense a healing taking place. The pain and heartache of the last few years was miraculously being drained away. God was already beginning the restoration process — and it was beginning within me.

Finding Forgiveness

Maybe you're thinking, "Pastor Dortch, I've done things, I've brought hurt to my family. I'm ashamed of myself. I got sucked into the power trap. I've sinned against God. I'm so sorry."

Let me tell you — from someone who's been there and back — God loves! God forgives!

I know now what it means when I quote the verse that says, "There is therefore now no condemnation to those who are in Christ Jesus, who walk not after the flesh but after the Spirit."

There is no condemnation! I am free, and you can find that release, too.

When repentance and truth merge, a dynamic comes into play, and God begins to open the windows of heaven. When we truly repent and give ourselves in humility to a loving heavenly Father, we don't need to make anything up to Him. When we submit ourselves to God and to others, we find true freedom — because we finally find ourselves.

> Let me lose myself and find it Lord in Thee.
> May all self be slain, my friends see only Thee.
> Though it costs me grief and pain,
> I will find my life again,
> If I lose myself and find it Lord in Thee.

NOTES

Chapter 1
[1]James Patterson and Peter Kim, *The Day America Told the Truth* (New York, NY: Prentice Hall Press, 1991).

Chapter 2
[1]Paul A. Cedar, *Strength in Servant Leadership* (Waco, TX: Word Books, 1987), p. 150.
[2]Mark A. Ritchie, *God in the Pits* (Nashville, TN: Thomas Nelson Publishers, 1989), p. 134.
[3]Robert D. Linder, "Pious Presidents," *Christianity Today,* February 17, 1989, p. 37.
[4]Stephen R. Covey, *The Seven Habits of Highly Effective People* (New York, NY: Simon & Schuster, Inc., 1989), p. 148.

Chapter 3
[1]David Halberstom, *The Next Century* (New York, NY: William Morrow and Company, Inc., 1991), p. 102.
[2]Charles Colson, *Kingdom in Conflict* (New York, NY: William Morrow/Zondervan Publishing House, 1987), p. 309.
[3]Ibid., p. 307-08.
[4]Tom Peters, *Thriving on Chaos* (New York, NY: Harper & Row, 1988), p. 628-29.
[5]Ibid., p. 629-30.
[6]Alvin Toffler, *Power Shift* (New York, NY: Bantam Books, 1990), p. 281.
[7]Peters, op.cit., p.630.

Chapter 4
[1]Peters, op.cit., p. 631.

Chapter 5
[1]Toffler, op.cit., p. 287.
[2]Mark Maremount and Mark Landler, "An Empire Up for Grabs," *Business Week,* December 23, 1991, p. 70.
[3]Ibid., p. 71-72.
[4]Charles M. Sheldon, *In His Steps* (Irving, TX: Word, Inc., 1988).

From the best-selling author of *Integrity*

FATAL

CONCEIT

How the Deception of **Power** *Becomes Every Man's Trap, Every Woman's Dilemma*

Richard W. Dortch

Former President of PTL

You have power over the lives of other people — whether it is your children, your spouse, or your co-workers. It's more than government officials, business people, pastors, or other professionals. It is us. Power unchecked can rise up and leave in its wake a flood of broken relationships, ruined reputations, and destroyed lives.

What makes ordinary men and women cross the line and misuse authority? Do we purposely set out to abuse our positions of power? How do we get sucked into the power trap?

This book identifies power personality traits, prescribes ways to avoid the pull of power, and reveals the use and misuse of authority. Dangerous tendencies could make you the next victim of fatal conceit. Find out where you stand before it's too late!

$14.95 - hard cover • $9.95 - paperback • $12.95 - audio

Available at bookstores nationwide or call 1-800-643-9535 for ordering information

Dear Pastor Dortch,

☐   I want to know more about Life Challenge.

☐   I need help. I have lost it all and want to find myself. I will be calling you.

☐   I would like someone to contact me for spiritual counseling.

NAME _____

STREET _____

CITY, STATE, ZIP _____

PHONE _____

LIFE CHALLENGE
Office Hours 9 a.m. — 4 p.m., EST
Phone (813) 799-5433

(Fold here — staple and mail)

```
┌ ─ ─ ┐
│           │
│   stamp   │
└ ─ ─ ┘
```

Life Challenge
P.O. Box 15009
Clearwater, FL 34629